Why Can Plants Grow in the Desert?

Written by Pierre Latour

Plants

Vital Vocabulary

2

Plants can grow in the desert because they can live where there is not much water. They can get the water they need.

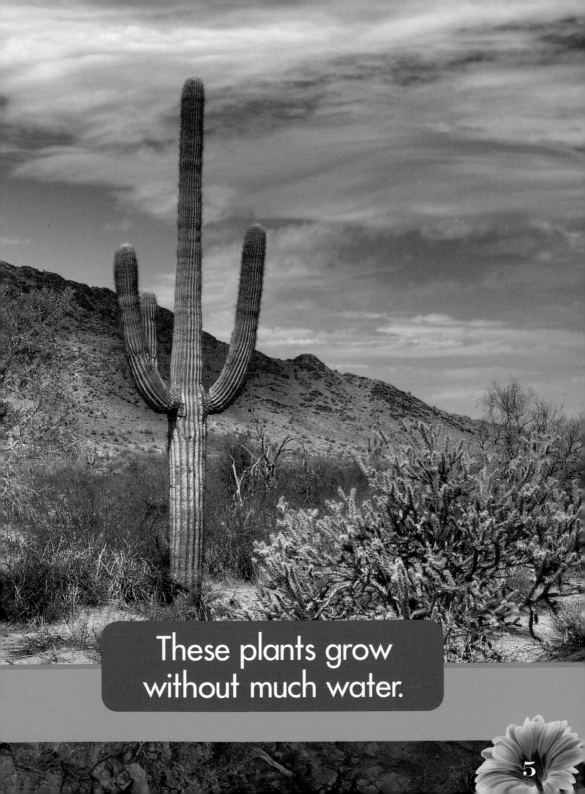

These plants grow
without much water.

This cactus can grow.
in the desert.
It has lots of stems.
It keeps water in its stems.

stems

This cactus has lots of stems.

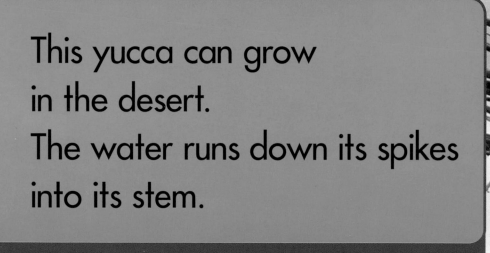

This yucca can grow
in the desert.
The water runs down its spikes
into its stem.

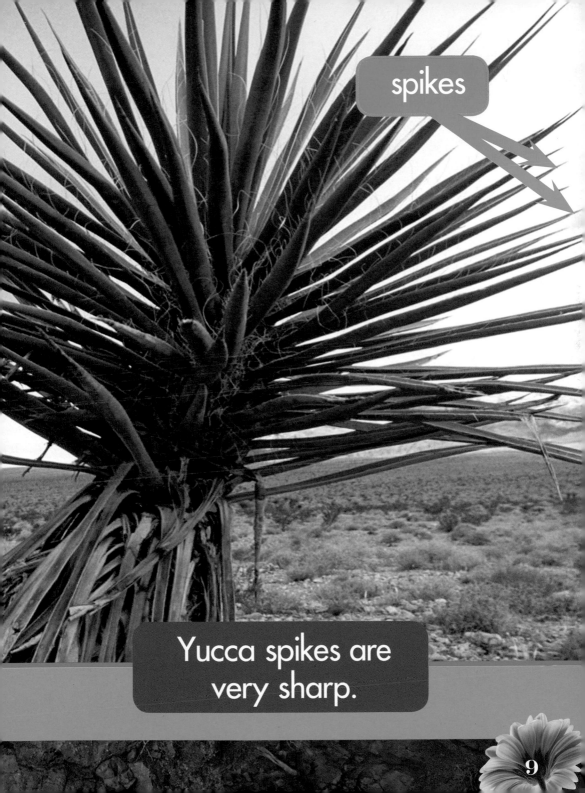

spikes

Yucca spikes are very sharp.

This mesquite tree
can grow in the desert.
Its long roots get water
from deep in the ground.

The mesquite tree
has very long roots.

This creosote bush
can grow in the desert.
Its long roots get water
from deep in the ground.
Its little leaves save the water.

little leaves

The little leaves close up to save water.

This ocotillo plant
sleeps when it is dry.
It wakes up when it is wet.

spikes

long roots

Ways desert plants get and save water

wakes up when it's wet

stem

long roots little leaves

Critical Thinking

Find out what this tree is.
How can it grow in the desert?